W9-CZV-659

America's Birthday
* * * THE * FOURTH * OF * JULY * * *

by Tom Shachtman * photographs by Chuck Saaf

MACMILLAN PUBLISHING COMPANY * NEW YORK

The author and photographer wish to give special thanks to the people of Camden, Rockland and Thomaston, Maine, and Portsmouth, New Hampshire, and to the following individuals: Richard Cutts, Claire Frye, Debra and Richard Longo, Loretta McGovern, Joseph Mayo and family, Rita Melendy, Bob Oxton, Doris Pike and, in memoriam, Marcel Lacasse.

PICTURE CREDITS: All photographs are by Chuck Saaf except the following: *pages 5 (top), 11 (bottom right), 14 (top left), 15 (top), 17 (top right, bottom left and right), 18 (left), 19 (top), 20 (left), 22 (bottom right), 24 (all), 27 (top), 28 (bottom), 30 (left), 40 (top), 42, 44 (left), 45 (left, bottom right), 46* copyright © 1986 by Tom Shachtman.

Macmillan books are available at special discounts for bulk purchases for sales promotions, premiums, fund raising, or educational use. Special editions or book excerpts can also be created to specification.
For details, contact:

Special Sales Director
Macmillan Publishing Company
866 Third Avenue
New York, NY 10022

Macmillan Publishing Company
866 Third Avenue, New York, N.Y. 10022
Collier Macmillan Canada, Inc.

Printed and bound in Japan
First American Edition

10 9 8 7 6 5 4 3 2 1

The text of this book is set in 12 pt. ITC Cheltenham Light.

The photographs appearing in the book were recorded on Kodachrome and Ektachrome transparency film, employing Nikon F3 cameras and lenses.

Library of Congress Cataloging-in-Publication Data
Shachtman, Tom, date.
Summary: The Fourth of July celebration along the coast of New Hampshire and Maine is presented in text and photographs.
1. Fourth of July celebrations–Juvenile literature. 2. Fourth of July–Juvenile literature. [1. Fourth of July] I. Saaf, Chuck, ill. II. Title.
E286.S5   1986   394.2′684′74   85-24207
ISBN 0-02-782870-0

The festivities to mark July Fourth begin at a gentle pace in the small towns and cities along the coast of upper New England.

1

The area is steeped in history, and many of its celebrations are rooted in tradition. In the days before the Fourth, the flags start to come out – a sure sign that the holiday is about to get under way.

2

The Declaration of Independence that was adopted by the Continental Congress on July 4, 1776, said that "all men are created equal" and that they have the right to "Life, Liberty and the Pursuit of Happiness." So a long holiday weekend in which everyone can celebrate the country's birthday seems appropriate.

3

For many, the Fourth of July is a good time for families to pack picnic boxes, load canoes or campers and gather to enjoy themselves. Some people take part in more public celebrations, and several of those are to be held this weekend. The Camden, Maine, firehouse has been scrubbed for the 103rd annual Firemen's Weekend. Down at the harbor, deckhands ready sailing vessels for the Great Schooner Race. On the grounds of the Strawbery Banke museum in Portsmouth, New Hampshire, the First New Market Militia Company sets up a demonstration of how soldiers lived in the year 1775.

And in Thomaston, Maine, on the evening of July third, volunteers prepare for tomorrow's day-long festival. "A lot of people like to celebrate," one organizer says, "but only a few want to do the work of getting everything ready."

The Thomaston Fourth of July party has been an annual event for almost a hundred years. The town has only three thousand residents, but as many as ten thousand visitors may come for the celebration. On this night before the big day, the talk among the Thomaston organizers – as among families all over the country – is full of small worries. Will tomorrow's weather be clear? Will there be enough hot dogs?

7

Near dawn, these weekend days, early risers start to cook for the crowds. In the Masonic Temple in Thomaston, at the Camden firehouse and on the Strawbery Banke common, people come together to share a traditional breakfast.

July Fourth is a unique time for Americans. Solemn memories of the past and deeply held convictions about the spirit of our country mix with the ingredients of a grand party.

In Thomaston, the morning's main event, the parade, shapes up along Route One. This year's theme is "patriotism," and garlands of red, white and blue seem at home in a place where history is part of everyday life.

Thomaston was named for John Thomas, a major general in the Revolutionary War; its most famous citizen, General Henry Knox, became the country's first Secretary of War. These men and others of their generation devoted much of their lives to making the United States a free and independent nation. Subsequent generations have redefined the spirit of the country. Their ideas are honored by floats depicting Uncle Sam, the Statue of Liberty and the "Four Freedoms"— freedom of speech, freedom of worship, freedom from fear and freedom from want – outlined by President Franklin Delano Roosevelt in 1941.

14

The main streets are lined with one- to two-hundred-year-old homes that once belonged to wealthy sea captains and shipbuilders. Before the Civil War, two of America's seven millionaires lived in Thomaston.

The parade is as much fun to cheer as it is to march in. Little Leaguers, beauty queens and local political leaders walk and wave proudly. When one band doesn't show up, another hurries through the parade route twice.

15

After the parade, the rest of the day at Thomaston is devoted to a grand variety of family games and entertainment.

Eat! Drink! Ride! Run! Throw horseshoes and baseballs! Dance! Make noise! Show off! This is a day for everyone to be outside and have fun.

At the childrens' pet show, each entry gets an award, whether it's for the "fluffiest cat" or the "smartest goldfish." Winners are interviewed for the local paper.

The all-day entertainment is free, and nobody minds eating a lobster roll or strawberry-rhubarb pie for a good cause. In Thomaston and elsewhere, many charitable and civic organizations use July Fourth to raise money for their activities by selling food, chances on prizes and home-sewn items that range from pot holders to stuffed animals.

19

At mid-day some people leave for the beaches, planning to return in the evening to see the fireworks. Others who seek relief from the hot sun visit the crafts exhibit on the Thomaston village green. A woman weaver offers handwoven fabrics that remind people of the past.

Clothes of an earlier time take on far more significance on the grounds of Strawbery Banke, in Portsmouth. Here, in one of the country's oldest continuously occupied neighborhoods, are several dozen restored houses that date from the seventeenth to the mid-nineteenth centuries; many are used not only for display but also as workshops for craftspeople. In that sense, Strawbery Banke is a "living museum" and an ideal setting in which to demonstrate what life was like during the Revolutionary War era.

Over two hundred years ago, each town or area in New England was responsible for its own troops of citizen soldiers. This weekend, modern volunteer units modeled after these old troops have come together to re-create an eighteenth-century military encampment at Strawbery Banke. The groups here are the First New Market Militia and the Coupon Company, both of New Hampshire; the Iroquois Scouts of New England; from Massachusetts, the Wilmington Minutemen and Artillery, the Newtowne Volunteers and, to play the British "Redcoats," the 9th and 43rd Regiments Afoote.

22

Their costumes and equipment are authentic, down to the last pewter button, and much of what they do is based on their own research. For example, they place straw around the edges of their tents because they have learned that old-time soldiers did so. The straw acts as a sponge and draws moisture, so the interiors of the tents remain dry.

23

24

Whole families have come to camp out, in imitation of the Revolutionary era when women – and sometimes children, too – traveled with the army. At that time, women were paid for cooking and cleaning in the camps according to the rank of the men they served. Boys in their teens left home to become recruits of the army and often took part in combat.

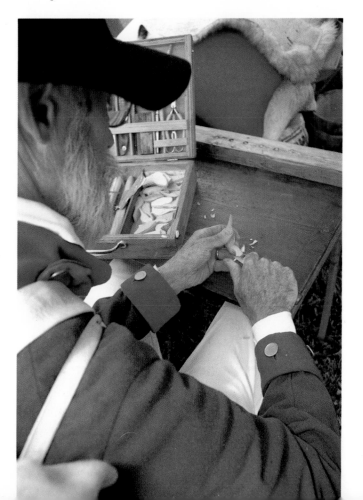

"Are we having fun yet?" Yes, they are, but for these people the hobby of re-living the past has become a passion. They say that learning about life at the time of the Revolution has made them appreciate keenly the dedication and courage of our country's first soldiers. Battles then were fierce and bloody, and many soldiers died from infected wounds or from diseases that ravaged the camps.

At Strawbery Banke, mock battles are settled with a laugh, but they also serve as reminders of the sacrifices of those who fought for this country's independence. Part of the purpose of the militia groups is to educate the public about the Revolutionary era. On encampments such as this one, visitors are encouraged, and during the school year the militia members give many lectures.

26

During a summer shower, the groups form up for a parade to honor an all-but-forgotten patriot, William Whipple. Before the Revolution, Whipple was a master mariner and businessman who lived in downtown Portsmouth. Then he went to Philadelphia as a member of the Continental Congress and was one of the fifty-six men who signed the Declaration of Independence, pledging "our lives, our fortunes and our sacred honor" in defense of the newborn republic. As a general, Whipple fought at the Battle of Saratoga. After the war, he was a circuit-riding judge, and finally came to rest in Portsmouth's old North Cemetery.

Farther up the coast, the seafaring tradition of the area is celebrated. Tall ships, most of them survivors of the age of sail which was at its peak a hundred years ago, gather for the annual Great Schooner Race from North Haven to Rockland, Maine. Sponsored by the Maine Windjammer Association and the Samoset Resort hotel, it's a competition in which everyone has fun, win or lose. To begin, the captains of the Coaster Class (pre-World War I) ships leave shore by jumping in skiffs and rowing to their vessels; first one aboard gets to weigh anchor before the others.

A lack of wind hampers the early going, but no one seems to mind. That's part of being at the mercy of the breezes and the waves.

Passengers help with the sails, perhaps imagining themselves as dorymen who once fished from these boats, or deckhands who sailed them as the schooners hauled lime, granite, timber, coal and ice up and down the Atlantic Coast. About fifty years ago, the great age of the schooners came to a close. As the ships were retired, some were refitted for passengers and for pleasure cruises.

The wind has picked up! The ships beat and
tack before it, picking up speed. They'll sail all
through the glorious day toward the finish line.

Directly inland of the schooners, in Camden, the sirens of dozens of fire engines announce the Firemen's Parade. Camden's Atlantic Engine Company Number Two was first organized in 1867. It helped fight the disastrous fire of 1892, when Camden was a center for shipbuilding and for woolen mills.

July Fourth has been celebrated in these parts as a major patriotic holiday since the time when our country was young. In 1840, for instance, people from Camden hauled a boat on a huge cart thirty miles up the coast to honor candidate William Henry Harrison, who was elected President later that year.

In this parade, the Knox Engine float commemorates more of the town's history; such engines were used for threshing grain, grinding corn and sawing wood at the end of the nineteenth century.

As the era of the great ships passed, the character of coastal New England changed. Between the years 1900 and 1940, Camden became a summer port of call for the wealthy. Now, tourists of all sorts come here to relax.

After the parade, the aroma of barbecuing chickens draws people to a lunch at the firehouse. The chefs are proud of their secret recipe. Firemen and their families come from all over the state to take part in this 103rd annual Firemen's Weekend, which includes a variety show, an outdoor church service, fireworks and a gala ball. It's a weekend-long party that provides visitors and residents alike with a sense of tradition and community.

As the afternoon sun begins to fade, people come to the great lawn of the Samoset Resort and walk out on the Rockland breakwater to watch the finish of the schooner race. The sail-powered ships of the Coaster, Leeward and Windward classes are cheered as they cross the line of the jetty. The first of any class to cross, and the winner of all categories of competition this year, is the *Mary Day*. Dinner and trophies await the sailors at the resort.

In the early evening at Thomaston, young and old gather for contra dancing, an old tradition that is kept alive in New England by singers and fiddlers. The dance came originally from France. It has evolved into a folk dance that mixes the stately gavottes of Europe two centuries ago and modern, foot-stomping, country square dancing. Such traditions are a reminder that the seafaring towns of coastal New England are only a few miles away from the still-vibrant farms of the area.

All along the coast, the day gives way to night.

At beachfront clambakes and at great parties,
sweaters and jackets come out to combat
the cool breezes. The air is filled, too, with
expectation – because the Fourth of July cannot
end without fireworks.

43

And the rockets' red glare,
The bombs bursting in air…

    Above town after town, explosions of color
light the night sky, directing some watchers'
thoughts to the glow of the past, as well as
to the present excitement.
    It is a fitting close to America's
44   birthday party.